NOBODY, SON OF NOBODY

NOBODY, SON OF NOBODY

Poems of Sheikh Abu-Saeed Abil-Kheir

Renditions by Vraje Abramian

HOHM PRESS
Prescott, Arizona

Cover design: Kim Johansen
Layout and design: Hope Sinatra, Hope Graphics

Library of Congress Cataloging in Publication Data:

Abu Sa'id ibn Abi al-Khayr, 967-1049
    [Poems. English. Selections]
    Nobody, son of nobody / renditions of poems by Sheikh
Abu-Saeed Abil-Kheir;
    Vraje Abramian, translator.
          p. cm.
    Includes bibliographical references.
    ISBN 1-890772-04-6 (pb)
1. Sufi poetry, Persian—Translations into English. I. Abramian, Vraje.
II. Title.

PK6451.A28 A23 2001
891'5511—dc21   00-054214

Cover art: Masoud Mansoori. Used with permission.
The couplet in the artwork is translated in this manuscript, number 62.

HOHM PRESS
P.O. Box 2501 • Prescott, AZ 86302 • 800-381-2700
http://www.hohmpress.com

This book was printed in the U.S.A. on acid-free paper using soy ink.

05 04 03 02 01   5 4 3 2 1

To Huzur

The Perfect Friend

ACKNOWLEDGEMENTS

My sincere thanks to Mr. Mosoud Mansoori and
Mr. Abdossalam Ahmed for their selfless support and
encouragement, to my wife Elizabeth for typing this
manuscript, and last but not least, to Regina Sara Ryan of
Hohm Press for her personal interest in and her skillful
editing of the original manuscript.

Remember to seek the
Beloved without the aid of
reasoning…one's own
intellect cannot be used to
comprehend one's own Creator.

Sheikh Abu-Saeed Abil-Kheir

CONTENTS

PREFACE

To those who believe in their teachings, "mystics" are living proof of that Eternal Presence that the human mind tries to freeze into time and space by giving it names such as Allah, God, Ram or Sat Purush. Throughout history, mystics have advocated personal experience of the Divine. They have maintained that humans have the potential to experience that oneness with the Infinite which lies beyond the realm of finite intellect. Such experience transforms the individual from one confined to the limitations and fears of self-centeredness, to a being who recognizes the presence of an Infinite Permanence somewhere in his or her consciousness.

One who is established in this recognition of Infinite Permanence is "free," in the sense that personal experience, not books or hearsay, make it possible for him or her to deal with the two issues forever staring the human intellect in the face: the issue of death, and the question of how to live life to the fullest. Personal experience with "The Infinite Permanence" reduces the issue of death to a mere change of venue, while providing a taste of some state of "Being" (or Non-being, perhaps) that prompts one to struggle for more of what makes life itself worth living! A Divine "drunkenness" of sorts now gives the individual the genuine ability to view life as a grand affair, too precious to be spoiled by such trivia as the amount of one's possessions, or the length of a lifetime, which is now appreciated as a temporary assignment within this Infinite Permanence.

For our mind to be convinced of the possibility of this grand affair, however, it needs the teaching and guidance of one who has experienced Infinite Permanence, and is a complete product of this experimentation. However, these teachers—the bringers of the message of genuine freedom—are not necessarily liked by everyone. Many of their number have been subjected to persecution, often instigated by those who found mystics' teachings a threat. This story has repeated itself several times in written history, and from all evidence it will continue doing so. Jesus in Jerusalem, Mansour Hallaj in Baghdad, Sarmad in Delhi were all persecuted by those who feared their message.

In Persia, after Islam was established, the term "Sufi" was applied to those remarkable individuals who demonstrated this message of genuine freedom and who acted as spiritual teachers. This brief book contains renditions of a few score couplets by one such Sufi poet, known as Soltan-al-Aarefeen, Sheikh Abu-Saeed Abil-Kheir. Iranian culture holds Sufi poetry very dear, in its heart of hearts. Perhaps it would not be too far-fetched to claim that, as a whole, this culture is based in a Sufi cosmology and worldview.

I have used the term *rendition* to underline the fact that the translations found here give priority to the content of the message, as understood by this translator, rather than any particular form, or word-for-word linguistic accuracy. In general, Persian (Farsi) cannot be considered a language that lends itself easily to English translation. Persian poems, of the caliber used by Sufi poets to guide seekers and to express their perceptions and states of consciousness, are often intense masterpieces of linguistic tapestry; mesmerizing plays on shades of meaning and the implications of these meanings in secular and spiritual realms.

To all Farsi readers who are perhaps used to "getting drunk" on the original versions of Sufi mystical poetry, and who may find more than a few shortcomings in these renditions, I have only my sincere apologies to offer. My purpose has not been to slight a tradition that has produced the likes of Bayazid, Attar, Shams and Jalal-eddin Rumi, but to make available in English, for the world reader, a small selection of some of the most refined expressions in human spirituality.

INTRODUCTION

How does one introduce a personality who demands to be spoken of as "Nobody, son of nobody"? Rather than focusing on biographical data, which may be obtained by referring to the sources mentioned in the bibliography, perhaps we can obey Sheikh Abu Saeed himself, and look into the life and times of this tenth-century mystic saint through his words and deeds. The anecdotes that follow are retold from an excellent book on Sheikh Abu Saeed, entitled, *Under the Sufi Cloak: Stories of Abu Saeed and His Mystical Teachings* by Mr. M. Jamnia and Ms. M. Bayat (Writer's Inc. International, 1995, used with permission).

Under this cloak is nothing but God.
Introduce me as "Nobody, Son of Nobody." [1]

Remember to seek the
Beloved without the aid of
reasoning…one's own
intellect cannot be used to
comprehend one's own Creator. [2]

Stories and Teachings

Master was asked how he had come to the mode of life that he was living. He replied:
"With a single glance from my Master, Pir Abul-Fazl … Everything I am, I owe to Him." [3]

Master read poetry and brought crowds into mystical joy and ecstasy. Some objected, saying that he left out the stern warnings in the Holy Book and spoke only of grace and mercy. Master said, "What has to do with us is all good tidings and mercy … " [4]

Sheikh Bu Abdullah Baku, lovingly known as Baba Kuhi Shirazi, was heard saying, "If I had not seen Sheikh Abil Kheir, I might never have seen a Sufi." [5]

Master did not eat until newly arrived visitors had been fed and comforted. [6] He always said, "Until you become an unbeliever in your self-identity you cannot become a believer in God." [7]

Master said, "Sufism is the ability of the heart to hear from God directly." He also said, "Put away what you have in your head, give away what you have in your hands, and do not shy away from what befalls you." [8]

One day a singer sang this poem in Master's presence:

I shall hide in my poem
to kiss your mouth
as you read it.

Master asked who had written this poem. "Amarah," they said. Master then visited this poet's tomb and paid respects. [9]

Master was asked about reason and intellect. He said, "This type of reasoning is a tool of the ego. Only beginners think about the secrets of the Path. Remember to seek the Beloved without the aid of reasoning, because one's own intellect cannot be used to comprehend one's own Creator." [10]

Master was walking one day with some followers in the bazaar of Neishapur. Some young men were passing by, carrying one man on their shoulders. Master asked who was the one they

were carrying. "King of the gamblers!" he was told. Master then
asked how he had become the king of the gamblers. "By
gambling and losing all that I had, without fear!" the young man
answered. Master exclaimed with joy to his followers, "Be
steadfast, lose all you have and become a king!" [11]

One Sunday, Master and a group of disciples came upon
a Christian church. The Christians had gathered for services, and
the disciples wanted to witness these. As they entered the
Church, the priest and those present recognized the Sufis and
came to greet them. There was much joy. Several Sufi *qawwals*
(singers) chanted love songs. Master's presence, and the love
chants praising the Beloved, brought ecstasy to all. When the
services were complete and Master prepared to leave, some
disciples exclaimed enthusiastically, "If Master desires, many
Christians here will give up their way and follow Islam." Master
said, "We did not bring them to that path that we should
presume to ask them to abandon it." [12]

He always said, "Anything which is not the word of God
is not worth discussing; while God's words themselves cannot be
uttered." [13]

It is said that a young man of means heard Master in a
gathering and was afflicted with that pain of which Master
always spoke. The young man sold his belongings and property
and brought all he had to the Master, who gave it all to the
needy the same day, as was his habit. The youth was ordered to
fast, repeat the mantram[*] given him and spend his nights in
meditation and prayers. For a year he was given the task of
cleaning the yard and the outhouse, for another he cleaned the

---

[*] mantram (or mantra): a sacred word or sound, often involving the name of
God, used as a form of prayer.

baths, maintained the furnaces for hot water and served the brethren. The third year he was given the task of begging for food, which Master then distributed as he saw fit. This went well. People in town admired the young man's steadfastness and filled his begging basket with bread.

After some time, things suddenly changed. The man was ignored and the public had nothing but contempt for him. Master also told the brethren to ignore him, and they treated him harshly every chance they had. But, Master himself was sweet to the young man, who bore his suffering patiently. Then, once again, this too changed. Master began ignoring him, treating him coldly, and soon hardly ever noticed him.

It so happened that for three days the youth was not given a piece of bread to break his fast, since by this time he was not being fed at Master's kitchen anymore. On the fourth night there was a gathering at the Khaneqah,* attended by a large number of guests. Many types of delicious dishes were offered. The young man arrived with an empty basket and an emptier stomach. Emaciated and weak, he made it to the kitchen, but on Master's orders, he was rebuked and thrown out. When he finally found his way into the dining room, he was ignored and left standing up near the door all night. Only after dinner had been served did Master notice him, severely chide him, and tell him how disgusted he was with him. He ordered the man out, telling him not to return, whereupon the man was seized by the Master's disciples and thrown out of the Khaneqah.

With no worldly possessions, no family or friends, no chance in this world, and no hope for the next, the young man was at the end of his rope, with no strength or desire left to hang onto it. He collapsed at an old mosque, and rubbing his face in the dust, he wept, "O' Lord, You know all and everything."

* Khaneqah is a Sufi gathering place.

You know how abandoned and forlorn I am. I have no one to turn to but You. All I want is deliverance from this wretchedness." He continued in this manner for the better part of the night. Then, suddenly, his burden was lifted and, feeling drunk and drowned in an unspeakable peace, he tasted that which he was seeking.

Just as this peace came upon the young man, the Master asked the disciples to bring a candle and, leaving the Khaneqah, they headed toward the old mosque. When they reached there, the man was still in that strange state, weeping tears of joy. "O' Master, what is this you have done with me, I am beside myself, vanished in this state."

Master said smilingly, "Is it fair to celebrate alone without inviting us? We have come to join you."

The youth's heart was still bleeding. Confounded, he asked his guide, "Master, how could you treat me that way?"

"My child," Master said, "you had given up all and everyone, but there was still someone between you and your Lord; me! I was the only idol left in the temple of your hopes, wants and fears and that had to be taken from you for your ego to surrender and take refuge in the Beloved. Rise now, let's relish this victory." [14]

When the time for the Sheikh's departure was near, he told those around him, "…this is what I was told by the Beloved: "I will soon take you out of the picture. So, all those who come to you will find Me there instead." Master also said, ". . . soon those who will lack loving obedience will be taught by the Lord directly."

"And who will these be?" he was asked.

"Those who will perchance ponder these words left behind." [15]

When Master was ready for his final journey to the realm of the Beloved, he said this in his last sermon: "When I

finished my studies with my teacher Muhammad Annazi and
was ready to bid him farewell, I begged him to forgive any
trespasses. In reply, he asked me the same, and then he bid me
never to forget God; not even for a moment. My last advice to
you is, do not forget God, not even for a moment. Know that
during my time, I did not invite you to myself. I declared that in
reality we do not exist. I say that He exists and that is sufficient.
He created us for non-being. Remember that a hundred years of
praying is not worth as much as making a heart happy. Walk the
path of God and see everything from His point of view. Look at
the created beings from the Creator's eyes." [16]

THE POEMS

2*   If you are in prayers in Mecca and your
      heart is elsewhere,
      you might as well be in an idol-worshipper's temple.
      If your heart is with the Beloved,
      spend your life in His wine shop and be merry.

3   Though burning has become an old habit for
      this heart,
      I dare not think of Your company.
      What would a moth mean
      to the fire that burns worlds?

4-5   Beloved, show me the way out of this prison.
      Make me needless of both worlds.
      Pray, erase from this mind all
      that is not You.

      Have mercy Beloved,
      though I am nothing but forgetfulness,
      You are the essence of forgiveness.
      Make me needless of all but You.

* The numbers assigned to these poems refer to numbers used in the original
Farsi version, *Arefaneha*. See bibliography.

6   If You order me to spend my life at the gates of
      monasteries,
      or have me running to Mecca,
      Your wish is my command.
      Glorious will be the day when You
      release me from my self.

7   Mansoor, that whale of the Oceans of Love,
      had separated his soul from the entanglements of
      this life.
      It was not him who claimed
      Ana-al-Haq (I am the truth),
      It was the Friend in whom he had lost his self.
      It was the Beloved.

13   Come back. Come back, no matter what you
      think you are.
      An idol worshipper? A non-believer?
      Come back.
      This gate, no one leaves hopeless.
      If you have broken your vows ten thousand times,
      Come back.

14   My Beloved, don't be heartless with me.
      Your Presence is my only cure.
      How can I be left with neither a heart, nor my Beloved?
      Either return my heart, or do not deny me
      Your Presence.

15   Sorrow looted this heart,
      and Your Love threw it to the winds.
      This is how the secret which saints and seers are denied
      was whispered into me.

16   All my deeds are dark.
      I am drawn in the river of my sins as deep as the Nile.
      They say the day of reckoning never turns dark.
      So it shall be,
      unless my deeds are brought to light.

17   Nothing but burning sobs and tears tonight.
No way out and no patience left.
Last night our hearts had a moment together,
I suppose this is how I have to pay for it!

18   Do not seek stability here,
seek no rewards.
You will be here a day, or five.
Seek to break no heart.

21   The day Love was illumined,
Lovers learned from You how to burn, Beloved.
The flame was set by the Friend
to give the moth a gate to enter.
Love is a gift from the Beloved to the Lover.

27   This frail body, bent under my heavy load of
dark deeds,
what if You hold my hand and walk with me, Beloved?
Though in my deeds You will find nothing deserving,
in Your Merciful Generosity there is everything I will
ever need.

30   One moment, You are all I know, Friend.
Next moment, eat, drink and be merry!
Another moment, I put every beast in shame.
O' Friend, how will this scatteredness that is me
find its way to You?

31   All my vows, You laughed at, on day one,
only to call me up on them, that eve.
You taught me to live with You, Friend,
with vows never made,
never to be broken.

33   Lovers are sacrifices to the Beloved,
and this world is their slaughter-house.
They find this world a royal feast,
while they are needless of food.
They desire no heaven, since without You, Beloved,
a hundred times higher than that is hell.

36   Piousness and the path of love
are two different roads.
Love is the fire that burns both belief
and non-belief.
Those who practice Love have neither
religion nor caste.

37   It is Him manifest in us,
all our struggles and achievements,
from that source.
Humility and meekness are appropriate here.
Before tasting the Presence, one rejects all that is
manifest.

38   A pious one with a hundred beads on your rosary,
or a drunkard in a tavern,
any gift you bring the Beloved will be accepted
as long as you come in longing.
It is this most secret pain,
this bleeding separation,
which will guide you to your Heart of Hearts.

39   To be in this imperfect existence for a moment
and to dream of Your eternal Perfection,
to have this heart full of wretched limitations
and to harbor this infinite pain of separation and
longing in it,
Your favors, Beloved.
All Your favors.

43   Detached You are, even from being,
and this being is nothing but You.
Unmanifest, yet the manifest is naught
but Your shadow.

Moons, galaxies and worlds drunk from this cup.
And the cupbearer is nowhere to be seen!

45   The deeper your involvement here,
the harsher your pain and suffering.
Donkeys with colorful ornaments and loud bells
are groomed for heavier loads!

49   The sum total of our life is a breath
spent in the company of the Beloved.

51   Whatever road we take to You, Joy.
However one is received, Honor.
With whatever eye one beholds You, Beauty.
In whatever language Your Name spoken, Joy.

54   Without You all creation is a prison—
heart, buried under mountains of pain and ignorance,
breath, out of tune, in disharmony,
life, so wretched, death itself will not receive it!

55   Life here is a gamble in which when you win, you lose!
Be content, that's how you beat the game here.
This world is like a pair of dice,
the only reason you pick them up
is to throw them down!

58   "This is My Face," said the Beloved,
wearing a basket of roses.
Thick, dark mystery flowing over the shoulder,
"This is my hair!"
A hundred musk incense sticks burning,
"This is My Perfume."
Fires everywhere, the whole creation aflame,
"This is My Passion."

59   Those who seek annihilation in the Beloved
      and poverty in life
      have no need of religion, knowledge or intellect.
      They do not even exist, only the Beloved remains.
      This is what the verse, "The poor have Him only,"
      means.

61   My Beloved, this torture and pain
      I suffer because I am so addicted to Your Beauty.
      People ask me whether I prefer Your
      company to being in heaven.
      Heedless fools, what would heaven itself mean
      without the Friend's Presence.

62   Your Creator, the Lord of All Creation,
      has given you two gifts, both sought after by all
      creatures
      your heart, the capacity to Love,
      The light on your face,
      the potential to be Loved.

65   Love came and emptied me of self,
every vein and every pore,
made into a container to be filled by the Beloved.
Of me, only a name is left,
the rest is You my Friend, my Beloved.

69   The one who knows the secret
is freed from his self and lives in the company of the
Beloved.
Negate your own existence, negate the self
and declare the Being of the Beloved.
This is what *la-ilaha-illallah* means.*

73   In your love, one lives without being.
I have cried my whole being away,
who then is this that still burns?
One who is trusted with inner secrets
loses his self in the Beloved.
Deny your self and be witness to the Presence.
This is what *la-ilaha-illallah* means.

---

* "There is no god, but God." *Quraan*, Arabic.

74   The Lover cannot live without sorrow.
Lack or abundance hardly matter.
Fortunate is the one who offers his life
at the first sight of the Beloved.

78   Suffering here is from wanting to be more,
to have more.
Peace and comfort are in contentment.
Choose poverty and modesty.

80   Be humble.
Only fools take pride in their station here, trapped in
a cage of dust, moisture, heat and air.
No need to complain of calamities,
this illusion of a life lasts but a moment.

81   The light on your face,
     you will take with you.
     All else, your sorrows, your joys
     and all that you lay claim on,
     you will leave behind.
     The light on your face,
     that you will take.

83   This corpse was given life,
     to find and fall in love with that Mystery,
     etched in sweet pain in the Living Heart.
     Instead you thrash around,
     sick and unfulfilled,
     seeking life from other corpses.

84   Seek no comfort in the realm of Love.
     This is where we lose all,
     and then some!
     You have come here, seeking a cure to all ills.
     Have you brought enough pain?

85 Drink from this heart now,
    for all this loving it contains.
    When you look for it again,
    it will be dancing in the wind.

89 What manner of a fool would try to sell
    broken pieces of glass for diamonds to an old jeweler?
    Don't display here the pain you haven't been
    blessed with.
    This is not the realm of pretensions.

92 Your faculties are for seeing through this flea-market,
    not to make it your kingdom.
    Seek contentment in the solitude of your heart.
    Soon there will be solitude only.
    What if you don't find your heart there?

93   Those branded with the fire of Love
      are free from temples and involvements.
      Having tasted the Real,
      they are needless of heaven, or hell!

96   A life, in which a single breath
      can contain all the universes,
      I have thrown away.
      My days, wasted in trying to figure out this blurred
      crystal ball,
      my nights, with shoulds and should nots.

97   A life-time spent in rushing,
      hair-splitting all along, without knowing.
      Though a thousand suns rose in my heart,
      the perfection of a single atom
      I could not fathom.

98   Let sorrowful longing dwell in your heart,
never giving up, never losing hope.
The Beloved says, "The broken ones are My darlings."
Crush your heart, be broken.

105   You have read but a page
and you fancy yourself beholding eternity.
Pages turn here rather quickly, be humble.
Only when actions bring forth the results of
your knowing, and you do not stray,
may you claim the first step.

107   Alas, in this school where sorrow teaches,
one has to bid farewell to many friends.
In this realm of pain and separation,
one has to bear seeing many faces fade.

115   Happy is the heart that blames none and
complains not.
Like the candle, it burns, melting to the last drop,
never giving up the flame.

120   If you want the highest this life has to offer,
never wish anyone harm.
Since neither is in your hands,
never fret over death, nor worry about life!

122   One day, this self, and all dear to it,
will be blown around in dust and dirt.
While you still have a chance, offer all you have here,
at this purifying flame, and be cleansed.
Garments torn, heart on fire,
let your whole being burn away in this Love.

123   A droplet of the dew on the face of this rose
called Love
fell on that dust which was, in the beginning,
to bring forth this clay doll we call our body.
The Love-tempered blade of existence tore
into the spirit,
bleeding a drop of light, which we call our heart.
Suns blazed,
worlds sang,
the grandest feat of creation was achieved.

124   The day I heard the murmur of Your Love—
mind, intellect, logic, I lost all.
After reading a page in Your book of Love,
I threw away all my books.

125   No one is sent away from Your door.
Those on whom Your sweet gaze rests for a moment
become life's eternal darlings.
Any particle which receives the light of Your Attention
becomes a thousand suns and more.

126   Lost in the fire of desire for the Beloved,
the Sufi dances in ecstasy,
to find a way to Him through the flame.
The wise know that the nanny has to rock the crib,
to bring calm to the screaming infant.

128   The secret of being stays ever hidden,
the shining pearl ever unnoticed.
Everyone brings his intellect into this,
so the real issue is never brought up!

129   Clouds in spring thunderstorms
have more permanence than our lives.
O' companions, live such that after death,
biting nails will be for those you leave behind,
not for you, dreading what may lie ahead.

130 When we were asleep in the nonexistence of before
the beginning,
before the coming of the regions,
before the erection of this turquoise-domed palace
of heavens,
Your Lovers were seared by Your firebrand
in absentia, Beloved.

131 Some argue destiny and free will unceasingly,
others negotiate rewards, garden palaces
with ever virgin concubines,
while yet others pride themselves
in the constant braying of their intellect.
Like the receding clamor of a caravan
leaving the center, fading into the ocean of this desert,
far, far away it all moves from this Silence,
which sits at Your gate, Beloved.

132 This eye that you use to gauge the fears of this world,
and hopes of the next,
is ill equipped to see the Lovers of the Friend.
They have given themselves up and are
released from here, and hereafter.
They are birds of a different aviary.

134   As long as you obey the vicious dog of your ego,
       the gazelle-natured ones will elude you.
       The hearts of the heavenly beauties
       are softened by your early morning tears only.

135   In school, tools are made available.
       In the company of True Lovers, eternal bliss.
       Where those true to themselves gather,
       integrity is distributed as alms to the needy.

136   We are filled with malice and ignorance,
       You are nothing but infinite subtlety in forgiveness,
       and dizzying delicacy in Love, my Beloved.
       With every love-filled movement,
       You create longing in the hearts of Your worshippers,
       O' Adorable Friend.
       Filled with the pain of separation
       the Lover longs for You at every step, Beloved.

139   Beyond imagination is Your beauty,
my perfect Friend.
How could I dream of Your friendship?
Beholding Your beauteous glory,
the Creator Himself takes pride in His creation!

141   Sometimes I am called a rosary—turning symbol
of piety.
Sometimes a devil-may-care drunkard in the tavern
of ruin.
Woe to me on the day when all pretenses fall
and I am called by the truth of what I am!

142   Rise early at dawn, when our storytelling begins.
In the dead of the night, when all other doors are
locked,
the door for the Lovers to enter opens.
Be wide awake in the dark when Lovers
begin fluttering around the Beloved's window,
like homing pigeons arriving with flaming bodies.

143 Those given to Your Love have no claims on life.
Having eyes for You only, they have long forgotten
themselves.
In the tavern where these single-minded ones drink,
the whole wine cellar is emptied and no one
loses his manners.

146 You knew what I would be like the day You created me.
I bring only my sins to You,
and this I do by Your decree.

147 I passed through churches and synagogues
and found everyone speaking of You.
With Your Love in my heart I entered the idol-
worshipper's temple,
I heard Your Name whispered while rosaries turned.

148   When destruction appears in six directions,
when all is annihilated,
your love-tamed heart will be the measure of your
worth!
Work on your love, be a human while there is still time.
On the day of reckoning only this will count.

151   Beloved, have pity on those who have none but You,
no thoughts but Your thoughts.
Forlorn and abandoned they are in life.
While in union, constant turmoil,
while in separation, constant pain is their lot.

153   How will your prayers and supplication bear fruit
if your head is full of crooked thoughts?
Demonic within, silk-robed outside,
how could fine dresses change your countenance?

157   Unless you turn your back to the world
       and close this shell of your heart,
       the pearl of understanding will not materialize
       within you.
       Your head is your begging bowl,
       it can't be filled with Beloved's alms
       if it is full of itself and turned upside down.

158   Beloved, if life itself abandons me,
       Your Thought won't.
       The reflection of the glory of Your Face
       has been etched onto my heart.
       This, neither life nor death can erase.

159   O' Delicate One of my dreams,
       what if You quench this thirst in this heart?
       What if You show this blind mind the abode
       of knowing?
       So many nonbelievers You turned into devotees,
       what if You teach this blasphemer how to pray
       in surrender?

160 O' Fickle One, with a thousand Lovers strewn around
Your courtyard,
my heart misses You.
When I say *God*, I mean union.
Pray hear my call.
Pray hear.

161 If I can find my way to You through hell,
I will pity all those in heaven.
And if I am taken to heaven and Your Love abandons
me,
I would leave that place of hellish lies.

164 Find the secret of your great good fortune,
and the priceless opportunity of this life
will not have gone to waste.
No matter where, who with, or what,
ever remember the Beloved in the privacy
of the Love Chamber of your heart.

165　O' Friend of the Fallen, untie this knot!
Only You can.
Have pity on me and this bewildered mind.
O' Bestower of Grace, I have nowhere to go,
do not send me away from Your gate,
O' Merciful One.

166　I asked the Bestower of Knowledge
Why have an eye?
"To stare with anticipation at the road where the
Beloved might turn up."
Why this mind, pain ridden, in agony?
"Then where would you store your love memories?"
Why this heart?
"What do you have in it?"
The pain of separation, the fire of longing for You.
"Cherish it.
Nowhere else, in all of creation, this is found."

167　O' Friend of the Fallen, have mercy on this poor one.
Do not allow my shortcomings to sit in my judgement,
but Your Grace and Mercy.
My existence is a mire of weakness and helplessness,
let Your Pity and Generosity pull me out of here.

168   If you taste every happiness here
every moment of your life,
if you spend all your days in the milky arms of
sweethearts,
death awaits at the appointed corner.
All of this is naught but a dream
from which you will wake up.

169   O' Ever Present One,
absent in the land of the blind.
O' Giver of All Wealth,
in whose Presence all pretense falls.
O' Singer of the Great Song,
unheard in the land of the dumb deaf.
All this creation tosses and turns
to reach that gift beyond all understanding:
consciously tasting Your Presence.

171-72 I have taken refuge in Your glorious court,
a fallen beggar in tatters.
You are all glory and grace,
I am all ignorance and resentment.
Confused and bewitched I am
fed up with myself.
With vows made and vows broken I have come.
Trusting Your Love and my wretchedness,
I have come.
O' Knower of My Sins Made, and yet to be made,
forsake me not.
I am nothing, you are the All.
I am at the end of my rope
grant me the trust to let myself fall.

175   O' my companion, my heart,
live consciously and die consciously.
Since your object in life is to reach the Beloved,
live on the road and die there, if need be.
Loving like this is living, otherwise in this
fakeness, formed
of our pretensions,
there's no living, only dying.

177   Since the day I saw Your Face
I neither work, nor fast or pray.
When You are with me
my blasphemies turn into sweet prayers.
When I am not with You, all my prayers
are naught but pretense!

178   Every dawn I bring my heart to You,
my lamentations are to soften Your Heart,
so You grant me the honor of being a beggar at
Your gate,
and no one else's.

184   Be amongst our friends and have no fear!
Be the dust at the gate of Love and have no fear!
If the whole world is out to get you,
rest your heart here, be ours and have no fear!

185   The essence of happiness you will know
when you discard all you hold dear!
Two beloveds in one heart won't reside,
if you want the True One, cross out all else.

188   Do not be mean.
Do not take when giving should be a priority.
If your needs make giving a burden,
then do not give.
Learn the way of the saw,
pull toward yourself on the way in,
on the way out scatter to the world what belongs to it.

189   If you are seeking closeness to the Beloved,
love everyone.
Whether in their presence or absence,
see only their good.
If you want to be as clear and refreshing as
the breath of the morning breeze,
like the sun have nothing but warmth and light for
everyone.

190   Are you seeking sovereignty?
Be a beggar, and a servant to all.
If you wish to be exalted,
be the dust under everyone's feet,
be a stranger to yourself and bear
everyone's pain.

191   Be an early riser,
seek the Beloved in your silence and solitude.
Do not let go of the One who receives you at the end.
Avoid all and everyone else.

192   My tears would flood the Oxus River
if my eyes didn't forever behold Your Vision, Friend.
Driven insane with the pain of separation,
my heart would sink in its own blood
if it did not float in the river of Your Remembrance.
I would devise a thousand tricks to spring my soul
out of the cage of this body,
if it did not insist on enduring this exile,
to arrive in obedience at her wedding with You, Beloved.

193 Raindrops might be counted,
but not my trespasses.
Sinking in the ocean of remorse,
in the depths of desperation,
I tread this valley of sorrows,
hanging my head low.
All seems lost.
Then I hear the Friend, my Beloved,
Ocean of Mercy and Grace.
"All is as it should be Darvish,*
you do what can be expected of you,
We will do what We are capable of."

194 Woe to me,
how can I blame the enemy
since I set fire to my own house?
I have no enemy but this wretched self.
Woe to me and my enemy self!
Woe to me.

---

* Darvish: one who has renounced; a fakir.

195   These lover's eyes have walked through
the book of love, page by page.
No face worthy of that Light, Friend.
No beauty worthy of this Love, but You, Beloved.
O Giver of Subtlety, You drown me in this Love
time after time.
I add to this book page after page.

196   You are my faith and salvation, Beloved.
Resting my head on the pillow of Your Love,
I sleep in this bed of longing.
How can a face glow such Love?
How can a heart survive such rapture?

197   It is the dark of the early morning, Friend.
All those thirsting after You have their foreheads
on the dust at Your gate.
O Beloved Source of the Water of Life,
pray order Your wine bearer
to water this pile of dust!

198   A hundred times a day I implore You
O Pure One, Absolute Creator.
I am a handful of dust, what may be expected
of such as me?
I know in Your Infinite Mercy one day
You will allow me to dissolve and join You.
In Your Infinite Knowledge and Mercy I rest,
with no fear of the world.

199   Someone asked me about the whereabouts
of the Heartless One, my Beloved.
"In my Heart of Hearts," I said.
"And where your heart might be?" I was asked.
"At His Feet."

201   If there were no human heart,
where would Love make Her home?
And what use would this heart be
were it not graced by Love for the Friend?
If you dare dream of reaching your Home of Origin,
the Abode of Perfection,
Suffer this separation in dignified patience.

203   I traveled paths of knowledge and
roamed regions of inner learning,
till I was recognized in the ranks of the knowers.
Once the curtain of ignorance lifted,
I realized nothing can be known.

204   Whatever I have written and said,
deserves to be forgotten.
Whatever I have gathered deserves
to be thrown away.
Whatever I have imagined knowledge
was falsehood and naught else.
In short, a precious gift of life was given, and I
have wasted it.

205   If I have committed naught but sins,
my hope rests on Your Mercy, Friend.
You told me very long ago
"I'll be there in the depths of your despair."
Pray, make Your word good, Beloved.
How can one sink deeper than this?

206   I have been crowned by misery and need,
nay, I am misery and need personified!
I am as poor and worthless
as my Beloved is generous and needless.

209   My hair has turned white,
all these years I have gathered
nothing but these dark deeds.
I had no perfumed incense to bring You,
I have brought You these dry sticks.
My boldness in entertaining hopes of forgiveness
and dreams of union
comes from Your royal decree, my Love.
"Despair is disobedience and shows lack of faith."

210   When the desire for the Friend became real,
all existence fell behind.
The Beloved wasn't interested in my reasoning,
I threw it away and became silent.
The sanity I had been taught became a bore,
it had to be ushered off.
Insane, silent and in bliss,
I spend my days with my head
at the feet of My Beloved.

211   Those who find me worthy of my name
have no idea of my inner unworthiness.
If I am turned inside out one day,
I would be judged to be burned at the stake.

213-14 Since the day I heard of You, my Love,
this confusion, sorrow and pain have never left me.
How foolish I was to think that we were two,
The Lover and the Beloved are never separate.

215   My body and soul come together to seek You,
it is You that I live and die for.
I am here but a fortnight and then,
a handful of dust.
You are here to see this Love through.

217   When I am on the road,
you are my bosom companion.
When I am in despair, my hope in hopelessness.
Whatever I do, wherever,
it is Your Face my gaze searches for, Beloved.

220   I can't leave Your door, Beloved.
I know this pain, this longing
will bring my end.
Pray remove this veil, O Creator of all Beauty.
Grant me a vision of Your Face beyond words,
or this burning I will carry to eternity.

221   O' cup bearer, do not stop this wine
or I'll be lost.
Here, everyone dies when his cup of life is full,
I know I will die if this cup goes empty
for a moment.

222   Hardships worry me not,
neither do all my trespasses,
I know there is forgiveness.
What I am afraid of most
is yet another separation,
when time begins anew!

223   The world to come
worries me not,
neither does death.
Why fear a true creditor?
What is to fear most
is the worship of this false self.

224   O' righteous ones,
please blame me not if I drink.
I worship this wine and the Love that goes with it.
When I am sober, I am in the company of intruders,
When I am drunk, I am in my Beloved's embrace.

226   Of all my infinite pains,
       and worse than this incessant burning in the chest,
       is the fact that You are sitting inside my very eye,
       and I cannot see You.

229   I look for no cure for this pain.
       With Your Beauty in my heart
       I look for no beliefs, no faith.
       When my time comes and I hear You call,
       I will worry not and turn in this
       wretched coin of a body
       to my Beloved, the owner of all treasures.

230   Ups and downs in my life
       are nothing but messengers from You.
       Joy and sorrow remind me of You only.
       I am so used to Your Presence, Beloved,
       Your absence is nothing but a reminder
       of the coming togetherness.

231   I am full of sorrow at Your gate.
      But I know the court of a generous King such
      as You, my Beloved,
      no one leaves wanting.
      I will be here therefore, my Love,
      until all my sorrows are
      sweet with anticipation and hope.

233   My Beloved,
      giver of all needs, and their satisfier too,
      pray see to it that I need none but You,
      and knock on no door but Yours.

234   Again I hear this song,
      and it smells of the wine we speak of.
      This is Your Sacred Secret, Beloved,
      declared in my heart, every moment.

237   Like the skin on a tambourine
resonating to the drummer's will,
this heart dances to Your Will.
When You wish, the whole world hears me,
When You want me silent,
a prayer-filled dome.

240   I did away with all wants
and likes spread across creation.
Only then could I love You
without the burden of this self.

241   Wining, dining and desiring
I also seek spiritual closeness.
This world of flesh and narrow needs
and that world of freedom in limitless expanses
cannot tolerate each other.
That's why I have neither.

242   For as long as there is a head on these shoulders
this is what it will contain:
Your Love is my ambition, pride, and achievement.
When these shoulders are no more to carry this head,
then it will rest at Your Feet, Beloved.

243   It's evening, there's no supper
and this heart is filled with contentment and joy.
My essence is fed from the beyond,
why should I care about
the who and what of this world.

245   Went to a healer to complain of this pain.
"Keep it as your sweetest secret," he said.
I asked for a potion to ease this tension.
"Your blood and tears," was the answer.
"What do I abstain from?" I asked.
"This world, and the next," he said.

246-48 Beloved, make contentment my wealth,
Your Love, the joy of my heart.
Let this creature of Yours thrive on You, his Creator,
make me needless of other creatures.
Make me needless of both worlds,
grant me that poverty You gift Your friends.
Guide this seeker in the direction of the secret victory.
Protect me from that which does not lead to You.
My Love, accept me to the inner circle of Your Lovers,
so I can share the secrets of their devotion.
Beloved, I am tortured by this tyrant of a mind.
Grant me the glorious lunacy of Love and
release me from myself.

249 This world and its joys and sorrows are passing.
Neither fathers nor sons possess
anything that they do not leave behind.
Spend this life in devotion.

251 Like the spring of everlasting life in absolute darkness
this creation protects the Secret it contains.
The ocean gives life to countless living creatures,
we see the living creatures and ignore the ocean.

252   You may bridge the shores of the galaxy.
       You may stop the creation from turning around
       its center.
       You may be able to control the snake and the scorpion
       but you will never be able to stop people from rendering
       judgments on you.

253   Love is not something one can talk about,
       this gem no diamond can cut.
       All we say and do are naught but speculations.
       Love comes undetected and leaves undefined.

254   This world and our life in it is worth nothing.
       We are nothing and so are our joys and sorrows.
       Is it smart to fuss over nothing?

255   Reject faces and places,
blow out the candle of your countless desires for a
moment.
I'll let you taste a drop of the
Ocean I am drowned in,
and you will live the rest of your days in bliss.

257   Cling to your poverty and refuse kingdoms.
Enter the dragon's mouth,
but seek not wealth here.
Sit in the silent solitude of the inner cell of your being
and dream not of palaces.

259   Your Love is the source of my joy and pain,
in Your Mercy, resolve this dilemma, Beloved.
Do not base Your Grace on the
worth of this worthless derelict,
do that which can be expected of You.

260   Your desires are legion,
while your wealth is carried off
through the ten gates.
Spend one night in purity and desirelessness
at the Beloved's gate.
If you aren't fulfilled, then complain.

261   Do not reject me because of my shortcomings.
Let not my troubles crowd my heart.
Do that which can be expected
of one such as You, Beloved.
Be mine today, and all tomorrows.

262   An idol-worshipping heathen
and a monk I am
of ill fame, a raving lunatic and
in love I am.
These, and a hundred times worse, I am.
Heedless, lost in the Ocean of Your Presence,
hidden from myself
and desiring to dissolve in You, I am.
But how can I reach You,
since in the essence and qualities
You are my hidden self
and I am Your manifest self?

264   The King dreams of his treasures,
the ascetic of his harsh, woolen robe,
lovers have nothing but this pain in their hearts.
Only the Friend knows what
He has hidden in their ruined chests.

265   The Mystery will always protect itself.
The secrets of before manifestation
neither you nor I will know.
Behind the curtain some are speaking of us,
but when the curtain falls, neither you nor I remain.

267   On the path of absorption
the irreligious and the pious both may journey.
Take a single step out of yourself
and see how clearly the path is marked.
O beloved of all creation, O human,
choose the way of surrender
and then if you wish
you may keep company with poisonous snakes.

276-77 All my desires and longings are made of You.
All my dreams and ambitions,
all my gains and losses, You.
The more I look at my days and nights,
today is all You and tomorrow will
all be You.
In my heart and soul
the one apparent and hidden is You.
Everyone's object of search in this world and
the next, is You.
You never leave Your solitude yet
with everyone You are always.
Ever solitary, always with everyone,
never expressible You are.

278 You play asleep these long nights
and I am missing You.
You play remote and distant.
This tossing and turning,
these long hot dry spells
and I am missing You.

279   His Love is the tamer of the lion,
and all else your mind might conjure up.
Now your companion, now burning
you in longing,
this friendship surely smells of blood.

280   All are confused and lost in Your attributes,
in both worlds, nothing worth doing but worshipping
Your Love.
You send the illness and You bring the cure.
In this coming and going nothing to count on but You.

283   One barters this life for public approval and position
to become a self-righteous, pretentious fool.
Another seeks traces of Your steps in his solitude
treading on the back of the dragon of lunacy.
You will spare none, my Beloved,
one will be slain by Your disdainful absence
the other by Your all-consuming Love Gaze.

284　You were pointed out the Beloved's mansion
and were shown the way.
You were told to clean your heart.
Colorful robes and turbans
are heavy loads on this road.

286　Without Your Name on my lips and
Your Warmth in my heart,
whatever I have done and wherever
I have been, I regret!
I vow not to take vows again since
in Your Presence I have broken
a hundred vows and repented
a thousand times!

287-88   To your mind feed understanding,
         to your heart, tolerance and compassion.
         The simpler your life, the more meaningful.
         The less you desire of the world,
         the more room you will have in it
         to fill with the Beloved.

         The best use of your tongue
         is to repeat the Beloved's Name in devotion.
         The best prayers are those in
         the solitude of the night.
         The shortest way to the Friend
         is through selfless service and
         generosity to His creatures.

289   Those with no sense of honor and dignity are best
         avoided.
         Those who change colors constantly
         are best forgotten.
         The best way to be with those
         bereft of the Beloved's qualities,
         is to forget them in the
         joy of silence in one's corner of solitude.

290 How can you ask for closeness
if all you have done has been
taking advantage of everyone?
Do not count on forgiveness,
your deeds cannot be considered undone!
The pretentious renunciate
is full of self-righteous hopes of salvation.
The remorseful drunkard,
assured of his worthlessness.
What if, at the end,
self-assured expectations and true
regrets undo the deeds
humans think God is a hostage to.

293 How long will you worry about this vicious world?
How long will you fret about your body?
The worst this world can do
is to take away this cesspool of
a prison your soul is trapped in.
Is that why you are worried?

294   Those seeking this world are
drunk of greed,
they will kill Moses and
worship the Pharaoh.
The covenant we made
with the Beloved before the beginning
is broken by greed in this dust bin.

295   Like vicious birds of prey,
we are all chasing our victims here
and fattening our egos.
When the day comes and all
coverings are removed,
we will see what it is
we have been doing.

296   O' Sweet-Faced Giver of Life
to all of Your creation,
each and everyone here is panting
for You and singing Your praise.
Woe to me if I am the only one
treated in this manner by You.
Woe to everyone if You treat
them all like You treat me!

297   I am the one You created from dust,
a handful of dust moving at Your wish.
You planted this seed,
this growth is obeying that command.

298   Who am I?
One with a fire burning within.
One with all hopes severed,
hoping to gain the steadfastness of a rock
and the sincerity of the flame.
Perhaps then I will deserve
to sit at the feet of the Purified One.

299   Who am I?
One fed up with his self,
at war with sanity.
One who burnt with jealousy last night
hearing the true lamentations of a truly
broken one at the Beloved's gate.

300 O' Creator of All the Limited,
Limitless One.
How long will You have this
derelict treading endless roads?
Pray, either remove all hope out of
this heart,
or grant the wish You placed in it.

301 You are either involved with the
highs and lows here,
or are busy sweeping the refuse.
How about a real loss? A true gain?
A complete chaos? An unbridled mayhem?
How long will you put up with this
repetitive boredom?

303 You took me in and pampered me,
allowed me into Your nuptial chamber
and watched my annihilation.
A hundred tricks to domesticate this wild beast,
and then cut it loose in this
half-scorched jungle ravaged by the insatiable
beasts of ego.

304   Cups of friendship and vows of
togetherness we exchanged,
then this cruel poison of separation.
Once I was no more, You asked whose corpse this was
and what he had died of.
O Heartless One, how can this be?

307-08 You granted me Love and
set me on the path of pain.
You freed me from logic and intellect
and took away my cleverness.
I was a man of letters sought by many,
now I am a footloose drunkard,
needless of anyone's praise,
unafraid of their blame.
Now poverty and contentment are my companions.
Friends, family and my own self
have abandoned me.
But this station You only honor Your Loved Ones with.
What service this unworthy one had rendered to
be exalted so?

309   You create these turning worlds,
these springs and winters.
You too send the righteous ones
to the bowels of the earth
while letting the beastly ones
steal crowns and thrones.

311   Do you know why the rooster
spreads his loud lamentations every dawn?
To let the living know
that another night has faded
into the mirror of morning light
and we haven't gotten
any closer to deserving the name human being.

313   Suppose you can recite a thousand holy
verses from memory.
What are you going to do
with your ego self, the true
mark of the heretic?
Every time your head touches
the ground in prayers, remember,
this was to teach you to
put down that load of ego
which bars you from entering
the chamber of the Beloved.

315   If you become popular
you are a true public liability!
If you run away from crowds
and hide, you are a trapped prisoner.
Better to know no one and be known
by no one, like Elias and
Khezr, the Loved Ones.

316   If you do not give up the crowds
you won't find your way to Oneness.
If you do not drop your self
you won't find your true worth.
If you do not offer all you
have to the Beloved,
you will live this life free of that
pain which makes it worth living.

317   Beloved, the two worlds are less than
dust at Your Feet.
Knower of All, to whose gate knowing
will never find its way,
if in Your Mercy you forgive all the living,
a handful of dust will find rest at Your Feet.

318   Friend I would throw this heart away
but it has Your fire brand on it.
Both eyes I would stitch shut if
You weren't sitting in them.
My whole being is nothing but Your abode,
or I would use it as incense
at Your door.

319   Though You are at the other end
       of the world, if I am in Your
       Heart, then we are together.
       Though You sit next to me, if I
       am not in Your Heart, You are
       at the other end of the world.
       Being together means not knowing
       that space where I end and You begin.
       where it becomes the same whether I
       am You, or You are me.

321   If you keep seeking the jewel of understanding,
       then you are a mine of understanding in the making.
       If you live to reach the Essence one day,
       then your life itself is an expression of the Essence.
       Know that in the final analysis you are that
       which you search for.

322-23 You are that Invisible Knower
who knows the secret pain of the lover.
Why should I worry about telling
You what I feel for You?
You know it a thousand times
better than I could ever express.
The trapped, wing-clipped bird's
longing for flight is nothing but Your pull.
You hear the flame burning in this heart
like a mother would know the
tears flowing down an orphan's face.

324-25 Beg for Love.
Consider this burning, and those who
burn, as gifts from the Friend.
Nothing to learn.
Too much has already been said.
When you read a single page from
the silent book of your heart,
you will laugh at all this chattering,
all this pretentious learning.

328 Building a thousand temples is nothing,
make a single human being happy.
Releasing a thousand prisoners from
captivity is nothing,
let true Love
captivate a single human being.

330 Until you have left all wanting,
all your loving smells of greed,
unworthy of the Beloved.
Until you have left your self,
and everyone else,
you will never be released
from this prison called me.

331 Beloved, pray do not make me
a refuge for the public.
Keep me at Your door,
needless of the beggar
and the King.
My black hair You turned white in Your Mercy,
pray let this face be worthy
of Your Light on it.

332 Crying a lifetime, and wanting You.
Running away from all and
taking refuge in You.
This derelict You have made out of me
takes refuge in You, from You!

333 What would you do with
this place of degradation and pollution,
this caravanserai* serving all manner of travelers.
Search for the One who is yours alone.
What can one who serves a hundred
thousand customers a day have for you?

338 In this prison house of ignorance
only sincerity in your desire to be
knowingly free counts.
Only sincerity makes you worthy
of the light of knowing.

* caravanserai: a place of rest, an inn.

339   In the school of mind you
       learn a lot, and become
       a true scholar for many to look up to.
       In the school of Love, you become
       a child to learn again.

340   On this path, first you will regret your being—
       you will be a heathen to all
       before, in this religion of Love,
       you are a being.

341   When you are annihilated by
       the eternal, you are
       released from the cage of this self.
       That which blocks your path
       is your boring self.

342   This world is nothing but a road,
heaven, a roadside inn.
True Lovers leave them behind
to reach the Beloved.

343   Until you have given up your
claims to ruling life,
neither this world nor the next
you will find peace in.
The day you bow to life in truth,
you will be nothing but peace.

346   Beloved, you live outside of *whats*
and *how manys.*
Happiness is to be Your Lover.
Honor is to have You as one's Beloved.

347　You are my Creator,
the Knower of my heart.
I am confused and stranded
on this road.
You map all destinations.
If an ant at the bottom of a well
begs You, You hear its cries.
Hear me, Beloved.

349　The Beloved is always true.
Whenever you become true
you will find Him.
When you become His in truth
and sincerity,
you will see, He always was yours!

350　I am the unruly, confused trespasser,
but where is Your Mercy?
My heart is dark,
where is Your Light?
You give me heaven for my devotion.
This is bartering, where is Your generous Love?

351 O' human,
     Hell is a flicker of your burning desire.
     Heaven a token of this divine Treasure, your soul.
     With Beloved's Love in your heart,
     live needlessly of both.

352 Creation in unison screams,
     "There is no one but the One."
     The worldly clever is busy trying to
     determine where he can cash in.
     The ocean's bosom heaves in Love,
     the floating twig takes the waves personally.

353 If you are a Lover,
     worry about none and own nothing.
     Rejoice in the promise of the Beloved that in this
     world, and the next, you have naught but Him.

355　O' foolish one, drunk of the wine of ignorance,
if you were not drowned in
your own blind greed,
you would not claim existence
in this place of death.

354　Like two points on the compass
we are separated when we are points,
though we have the same body.
My Love, we are now two points separated,
when this is done and accomplished,
we will merge back again.
One being.

ENDNOTES

1. Jamia, M.A. and Mojdeh Bayat. *Under the Sufi Cloak.*
    Beltsville, Maryland: Writers' Inc. International, 1995, xi.
2. Ibid., 51.
3. Graham, Terry. "Abu Sa'id ibn Abi'l-Khayer and the
    School of Khurasan," in *Classical Persian Sufism from
    Origins to Rumi*, ed. Leonard Lewisohn. London:
    Khaniqahi Nimatu Ullahi Publications (KNP), 1993, 89.
4. Ibid., 119.
5. Ibid., 120.
6. Ibid., 124.
7. Ibid., 129.
8. Jamnia and Bayat, 33 and 118.
9. Ibid., 37.
10. Ibid., 51.
11. Ibid., 35.
12. Ibid., 53.
13. Ibid., 16.
14. Neishapuri, Arrat, Sheikh Farideddin. *Tazkarat-ol-Oliya.*
    (*Biographies of the Saints*). Dr. Mahmmad Estelami, ed.
    Tehran, Iran: Zavvar Publications, original Farsi version,
    1994. 807-809.
15. Ibid., 814.
16. Jamnia and Bayat, 31.

BIBLIOGRAPHY

Masoomi, Reza. *Arefaneha, Jami az Oqianoose Beekarane Erfan (Selections of Mystic Poetry, a Cup from the Infinite Ocean of Gnosi)* 6th Edition. Tehran, Iran: Nashre-Eshare Publications, 1991. (Original Farsi version). Notes from selected pages 17-88.

Further Reading:

Monavvar, M. *The Secrets of God's Mystical Oneness.* Translated by John O'Kane. Los Angeles: Mazda Publications, 1992.

ADDITIONAL TITLES FROM HOHM PRESS

RENDING THE VEIL: Literal and Poetic Translations of Rumi
by Shahram T. Shiva
Preface by Peter Lamborn Wilson

With a groundbreaking transliteration, English-speaking lovers of Rumi's poetry will have the opportunity to "read" his verse aloud, observing the rhythm, the repetition, and the rhyme that Rumi himself used over 800 years ago. Offers the reader a hand at the magical art of translation, providing a unique "word by word" literal translation from which to compose one's own variations. Together with exquisitely-rendered Persian calligraphy of 252 of Rumi's quatrains (many previously untranslated), Mr. Shiva presents his own poetic English version of each piece. From his study of more than 2000 of Rumi's short poems, the translator presents a faithful cross-section of the poet's many moods, from fierce passion to silent adoration.

Cloth, 280 pages, $27.95   ISBN: 0-93425246-7

...

RUMI — *THIEF OF SLEEP*
180 Quatrains from the Persian
Translations by Shahram Shiva
Foreword by Deepak Chopra

This book contains 180 translations of Rumi's short devotional poems, or *quatrains*. Shiva's versions are based on his own carefully documented translation from the Farsi (Persian), the language in which Rumi wrote.

"In *Thief Of Sleep*, Shahram Shiva (who embodies the culture, the wisdom and the history of Sufism in his very genes) brings us the healing experience. I recommend his book to anyone who wishes *to remember*. This book will help you do that."—Deepak Chopra, author of *How to Know God*

Paper, 120 pages, $11.95   ISBN:1-890772-05-4

TO ORDER PLEASE SEE ACCOMPANYING ORDER FORM
OR CALL 1-800-381-2700 TO PLACE YOUR ORDER NOW.

ADDITIONAL TITLES FROM HOHM PRESS

CRAZY AS WE ARE
Selected Rubais from the Divan-i-Kebir of Mevlana Celaleddin Rumi
Introduction and Translation by Dr. Nevit O. Ergin

This book is a collection of 128 previously untranslated *rubais*, or quatrains (four-line poems which express one complete idea), of the 13th-century scholar and mystic poet Rumi. Filled with the passion of both ecstasy and pain, Rumi's words may stir remembrance and longing, or challenge complacency in the presence of awesome love. Ergin's translations (directly from Farsi, the language in which Rumi wrote) are fresh and highly sensitive, reflecting his own resonance with the path of annihilation in the Divine as taught by the great Sufi masters.

Paper, 88 pages, $9.00   ISBN 0-934252-30-0

· · ·

IN PRAISE OF RUMI
Lee Lozowick, and others
Introduction by Regina Sara Ryan

Once a great Turkish scholar and theologian, Jelaluddin Rumi lost his heart to a wandering beggar, Shams E Tabriz, in whom he saw the face of God. His poetry extols his love and longing—for his beloved teacher, and for the Divine, alive in all things. *In Praise of Rumi* is a book of ecstatic poetry. It is an expression from the same chamber of the heart in which Rumi danced over 700 years ago. A book for those who know what it means to have a wounded heart, *In Praise of Rumi* celebrates the bittersweet pain and pleasure of tasting the raw Divine.

Paper, 80 pages, $8   ISBN: 0-934252-23-8.

TO ORDER PLEASE SEE ACCOMPANYING ORDER FORM
OR CALL 1-800-381-2700 TO PLACE YOUR ORDER NOW.

ADDITIONAL TITLES FROM HOHM PRESS

THE MIRROR OF THE SKY
Songs of the Bauls of Bengal
Translated by Deben Bhattacharya

Baul music today is prized by world musicologists, and Baul lyrics are treasured by readers of ecstatic and mystical poetry. Their music, lyrics and accompanying dance reflect the passion, the devotion and the iconoclastic freedom of this remarkable sect of musicians and lovers of the Divine, affectionately known as "God's troubadours."

The Mirror of the Sky is a translation of 204 songs, including an extensive introduction to the history and faith of the Bauls, and the composition of their music. It includes a CD of authentic Baul artists, recorded as much as forty years ago by Bhattacharya, a specialist in world music. The current CD is a rare presentation of this infrequently documented genre.

Paper, 288 pages, $24.95 (includes CD)   ISBN: 0-934252-89-0
CD sold separately, $16.95

• • •

SONGS OF THE QAWALS OF INDIA
Islamic Lyrics of Love and God
Recordings by Deben Bhattacharya

These recent recordings of a centuries-old musical form were made in Kashmir and in Varanasi, India. Five exquisite songs speak of love, life and death, of God and the dedicated beings, of the Prophet Muhammad and his early followers.

Qawali in its current musical form was introduced in India towards the end of the 13th century by a great musician named Amir Khasru, whose ancestors came to India from Iran. The name Qawali is also attributed to a rhythm of eight beats, divided 4/4. Qawali is sung in both Hindi- and Urdu-speaking regions of North India, usually by professional Muslim Qawals (singers), while the musicians are generally Hindus. The instruments used are those popular with the folk musicians of North India: the harmonium, the *sarangi* or broad-necked fiddle, the barrel-shaped double-headed drum (*dholak*) and a pair of cymbals.

Includes photos, introduction and song lyrics
60-minute CD, $15.00   ISBN: 1-890772-12-7

**TO ORDER PLEASE SEE ACCOMPANYING ORDER FORM
OR CALL 1-800-381-2700 TO PLACE YOUR ORDER NOW.**

ADDITIONAL TITLES FROM HOHM PRESS

GRACE AND MERCY IN HER WILD HAIR
Selected Poems to the Mother Goddess
Ramprasad Sen; Translated by Leonard Nathan and Clinton Seely

Ramprasad Sen, a great devotee of the Mother Goddess, composed these passionate poems in 18th-century Bengal, India. His lyrics are songs of praise or sorrowful laments addressed to the great goddesses Kali and Tara, guardians of the cycles of birth and death.

Paper, 96 pages, $12   ISBN: 0-934252-94-7

• • •

FOR LOVE OF THE DARK ONE: Songs of Mirabai
Revised edition
Translations and Introduction by Andrew Schelling

Mirabai is probably the best known poet in India today, even though she lived 400 years ago (1498-1593). Her poems are ecstatic declarations of surrender to and praise to Krishna, whom she lovingly calls "The Dark One." Mira's poetry is as alive today as if was in the sixteenth century—a poetry of freedom, of breaking with traditional stereotypes, of trusting completely in the benediction of God. It is also some of the most exalted mystical poetry in all of world literature, expressing her complete surrender to the Divine, her longing, and her madness in love. This revised edition contains the original 80 poems, a completely revised Introduction, updated glossary, bibliography and discography, and additional Sanskrit notations.

Paper, 128 pages, $12.00   ISBN: 0-934252-84-X

TO ORDER PLEASE SEE ACCOMPANYING ORDER FORM OR CALL 1-800-381-2700 TO PLACE YOUR ORDER NOW.

ADDITIONAL TITLES FROM HOHM PRESS

MARROW OF FLAME: Poems of the Spiritual Journey
by Dorothy Walters
Foreword by Andrew Harvey

This compilation of 105 new poems documents and celebrates the author's interior journey of *kundalini* awakening. Her poems cut through the boundaries of religious provincialism to the essence of longing, love and union that supports every authentic spiritual tradition, as she writes of the Mother Goddess, as well as of Krishna, Rumi, Bodhidharma, Hildegard of Bingen, and many others.Best-selling spiritual author and poet Andrew Harvey has written the book's Introduction. His commentary illuminates aspects of Dorothy's spiritual life and highlights the "unfailing craft" of her poems.

"Dorothy Walters writes poetry that speaks to us from the heart to the heart, gently touching our deepest spiritual stirrings."—Riane Eisler, author, *The Chalice and the Blade.*

Paper, 144 pages, $12.00   ISBN: 0-934252-96-3

· · ·

THE ART OF DYING
RedHawk

RedHawk's poetry cuts close to the bone whether he is telling humorous tales or indicting the status-quo throughout the culture. Touching upon themes of life and death, power, devotion and adoration, these ninety new poems reveal the poet's deep concern for all of life, and particularly for the needs of women, children and the earth.

"An eye-opener; spiritual, native, populist. RedHawk's is a powerful, wise, and down-home voice."—Gary Snyder

Paper, 120 pages, $12   ISBN: 0-934252-93-9

TO ORDER PLEASE SEE ACCOMPANYING ORDER FORM OR CALL 1-800-381-2700 TO PLACE YOUR ORDER NOW.

ADDITIONAL TITLES FROM HOHM PRESS

WOMEN CALLED TO THE PATH OF RUMI
The Way of the Whirling Dervish
by Shakina Reinhertz

This is the first English-language book to share the experience of Turning by women practitioners of the Mevlevi Order of Whirling Dervishes. It outlines the history of the women who have followed this way since Rumi's time, illuminates the transmission of this work from Turkey to America, and highlights the first twenty years of the Order's life in a new country and culture.

The heart of the book is the personal experience of contemporary women—interviews with over two dozen American initiates (from adolescents to wise elders), many of whom have practiced on this path for twenty years or more. Their descriptions of the rituals and ceremonies of the Mevlevi way are offered from the viewpoint of the participant rather than the observer.

"I love the wisdom and fire of this book. It's full of the light of longing and people trying to experience the mystery of that truth."—Coleman Barks, author, and translator of Rumi's poetry

Paper, 300 pages, $23.95   ISBN: 1-890772-04-6
240 black and white photos and illustrations

• • •

NOBODY SON OF NOBODY
Poems of Shaikh Abu-Saeed Abil-Kheir
Renditions by Vraje Abramian

Anyone who has found a resonance with the love-intoxicated poetry of Rumi, must read the poetry of Shaikh Abil-Kheir. This renowned, but little known Sufi mystic of the 10th century preceded Rumi by over two hundred years on the same path of annihilation into God. This book contains translations and poetic renderings of 195 short selections from the original Farsi, the language in which Abil-Kheir wrote.

These poems deal with the longing for union with God, the desire to know the Real from the false, the inexpressible beauty of creation when seen through the eyes of Love, and the many attitudes of heart, mind and feeling that are necessary to those who would find the Beloved, The Friend, in this life.

Paper, 120 pages, $12.95   ISBN: 1-890772-04-6

TO ORDER PLEASE SEE ACCOMPANYING ORDER FORM
OR CALL 1-800-381-2700 TO PLACE YOUR ORDER NOW.

RETAIL ORDER FORM FOR HOHM PRESS BOOKS

Name_____ Phone (   ) _____

Street Address or P.O. Box _____

City _____ State _____ Zip Code _____

	QTY	TITLE	ITEM PRICE	TOTAL PRICE
	1	**THE ART OF DYING**	$12.00	
	2	**CRAZY AS WE ARE**	$9.00	
	3	**FOR LOVE OF THE DARK ONE**	$12.00	
	4	**GRACE AND MERCY IN HER WILD HAIR**	$12.00	
	5	**IN PRAISE OF RUMI**	$8.00	
	6	**MARROW OF FLAME**	$12.00	
	7	**MIRROR OF THE SKY, INCLUDES CD**	$24.95	
	8	**MIRROR OF THE SKY, CD ONLY**	$16.95	
	9	**NOBODY SON OF NOBODY**	$12.95	
	10	**RENDING THE VEIL**	$27.95	
	11	**RUMI—THIEF OF SLEEP**	$11.95	
	12	**SONGS OF THE QAWALS OF INDIA**	$15.00	
	13	**WOMEN CALLED TO THE PATH OF RUMI**	$23.95	

SURFACE SHIPPING CHARGES

1st book $5.00

Each additional item $1.00

SUBTOTAL: _____

SHIPPING: (see below) _____

TOTAL: _____

SHIP MY ORDER

☐ Surface U.S. Mail—Priority   ☐ UPS (Mail + $2.00)

☐ 2nd-Day Air (Mail + $5.00)   ☐ Next-Day Air (Mail + $15.00)

METHOD OF PAYMENT:

☐ Check or M.O.   Payable to Hohm Press, P.O. Box 2501, Prescott, AZ 86302

☐ Call 1-800-381-2700 to place your credit card order

☐ Or call 1-520-717-1779 to fax your credit card order

☐ Information for Visa/MasterCard/American Express order only:

Card #_____ – _____ – _____ – _____   Expiration Date _____

Visit our Website to view our complete catalog: www.hohmpress.com

ORDER NOW! Call 1-800-381-2700 or fax your order to 1-520-717-1779.

(Remember to include your credit card information.)